W9-BJP-458

JOHNNY APPLESEED

Troll Associates

JOHNNY APPLESEED

by Louis Sabin

Illustrated by Dick Smolinski

Troll Associates

Library of Congress Cataloging in Publication Data

Sabin, Louis.
   Johnny Appleseed.

   Summary: A brief biography of John Chapman, who for
nearly fifty years wandered the Midwest, planting apple-
seeds and spreading the word of God.
   1. Appleseed, Johnny, 1774-1845—Juvenile literature.
2. Apple growers—United States—Biography—Juvenile
literature.   3. Missionaries—United States—Biography—
Juvenile literature.   4. Frontier and pioneer life—Middle
West—Juvenile literature.   [1. Appleseed, Johnny, 1774-
1845.   2. Apple growers.   3. Missionaries.   4. Frontier
and pioneer life—Middle West]   I. Smolinski, Dick, ill.
II. Title.
SB63.C46S33   1985   634'.11'0924 [B] [92]   84-2732
ISBN 0-8167-0220-9 (lib. bdg.)
ISBN 0-8167-0221-7 (pbk.)

Greatness is a word often used in describing presidents who lead a nation through times of crisis, generals who win important battles, and scientists who make remarkable discoveries. But there is another kind of greatness. It doesn't earn headlines or huge financial rewards. It is the quiet, unselfish work of a person who is totally dedicated to doing good. That kind of greatness belonged to John Chapman, better known as Johnny Appleseed.

7

There are so many stories about Johnny Appleseed that sometimes it's hard to separate the facts from the legends. We do know that John Chapman was born in Leominster, Massachusetts on September 26, 1774. His father, Nathaniel, owned a small farm there and also did some carpentry.

In 1775, when Johnny was just a few months old, his father joined the Minutemen and went off to fight in the Revolutionary War. The Minutemen were volunteers who believed that the American Colonies should be independent of Britain. As he grew up, Johnny was always proud of the role his father played in the American Revolution.

In 1776, when Johnny was just two years old, his mother died. From then until his father was released from military service, four years later, the boy was taken care of by relatives. These relatives made sure that he was fed and clothed, but they didn't give him the close attention and love of parents.

Johnny spent a great deal of time alone, roaming the woods around Leominster. He felt most comfortable away from people, watching the animals and birds and learning about flowers and trees and insects. Even as a child, Johnny was never afraid of any wild animal. And the forest creatures seemed to sense that he was a friend.

When Nathaniel Chapman came home from the war, he married again. In time, Johnny had ten sisters and brothers. His stepmother was busy with all of her young children. And his father gave all his attention to farming. Nobody gave much time to Johnny. As lonely as before, the boy continued to spend his days in the nearby woods.

Wherever Johnny went he carried his Bible. He was deeply religious. Johnny wanted to spread his faith to others and to share with people the beauty of the world as he saw it. To him, the bounty of nature was the gift of God.

Sometime in his teen years, John Chapman became especially interested in growing apple trees. Nobody really knows how this came about. Some historians think that John developed this interest while working in a neighbor's orchard.

Others believe that Johnny had religious reasons for his work with apples. Still others say that by planting apple trees, Johnny was simply continuing an early American tradition.

The first settlers in the New World had brought apple seeds from England. And every colony in America was filled with orchards. Thomas Jefferson and George Washington had large apple orchards on their properties. There was an orchard in Virginia that had eight different kinds of apple trees—2,500 trees in all!

The apple was a very important product in early America. The fruit itself was used for apple butter, jelly, preserves, cider, brandy, dried apples, and vinegar. It was baked in pies, cooked with meat, or eaten raw. The hardwood of apple trees was used for tools and furniture or burned as fragrant firewood.

Best of all, apple trees grew well in every colony and in all kinds of soil. And apples did not spoil easily. So they could be kept in a cool place all winter. That way they provided fresh food all year long.

Apples had another significance to the settlers. Apple trees represented permanence. It takes time for a seed to grow into a tree and produce fruit. People do not usually plant fruit trees unless they intend to stay in one place for a long time. Some settlements in Ohio made apple orchards a requirement for land title. That is, anyone who wanted title to a piece of property had to plant fifty apple trees within three years of moving onto the land.

19

John Chapman knew the value of apples to the pioneers. So he put his faith in apple seeds when he left Massachusetts in 1797. During that winter, John Chapman walked all over the Allegheny Valley in western Pennsylvania. He wanted to start a nursery of apple trees, and he was looking for a good location.

In order to survive that winter, Johnny used his vast knowledge of the outdoors. He had almost no money and little more than the clothing that he wore. He made protection for his feet from a shirt and snowshoes from the supple branches of a young beech tree. His diet was made up of nuts, dried berries, and whatever else he could find in the winter woods.

When Johnny was thirsty he made tea from fennel leaves. Fennel is an herb of the carrot family. Johnny believed that this herb tea acted as a medicine against fever and chills. Throughout his life, along with the apple trees he planted, Johnny scattered fennel seeds. It is also said that Johnny distributed Norway-spruce seedlings and the seeds of red day lilies to settlers.

During the spring of 1798, John Chapman started his first apple-tree nursery on a small piece of land near the Allegheny River. He got his apple seeds for free—from nearby cider mills. The mills always threw away the seeds from the apples they pressed into cider.

Chapman remained in western Pennsylvania for the next three or four years. When the seeds he planted began to produce seedlings, Johnny tried to sell them. Those he could not sell, he gave away. It was more important to Johnny to see apple trees grow than to make money.

Then Johnny moved on again—traveling west and planting apple seeds wherever he went. Records show that John Chapman cleared plots of land and established apple-tree nurseries thirty-four times over the next forty-three years.

John Chapman spent most of his adult life wandering around Ohio and Indiana, selling apple seedlings and scattering seeds. He also handed out religious pamphlets and preached sermons to anyone who would listen.

Winter and summer, Johnny wore the same ragged shirt and pants. These were made from rough cloth or animal skins the Indians gave him. And no matter what the weather was, he went barefooted and carried everything he owned in a large bag slung over one shoulder. The bag contained seeds, plants, his Bible, and religious pamphlets.

John Appleseed, as the midwestern settlers came to call him, usually appeared at a settler's cabin toward evening. First, he sold or gave some seeds or seedlings to the family. Then he shared their evening meal, but never ate any meat. In the early years of his wandering, John ate indoors with the settlers. But as he grew older, he took the food given him and ate it outside. He also preferred to sleep outdoors or in a hayloft.

After supper, John preached his sermon. He talked about God and nature and the wonders of animals and plants. The children enjoyed Chapman's sermons. They listened for hours as he recounted his adventures and described some of the marvelous things he had seen.

The midwestern Indians also welcomed Johnny Appleseed into their dwellings. They fed him and saw that no harm came to him. More than once, Chapman learned of a planned Indian raid and warned the settlers. But the Indians still gave him complete freedom to come and go among them.

In March of 1845, John Chapman was somewhere in Indiana when he heard that cattle were trampling his apple-tree nursery near Fort Wayne. He immediately set out for the nursery. But by the time he arrived, the seventy-year-old naturalist had pneumonia. A settler named William Worth took him in and tried to restore his health. It was too late, and John Chapman died within a few days.

The man called Johnny Appleseed was buried somewhere in Fort Wayne, but nobody knows where. Many years later, the city erected a memorial stone in his honor. On it are the simple words: "He lived for others."

Today, the legacy of Johnny Appleseed can be seen throughout the midwestern United States. Thousands and thousands of apple trees, Norway spruce, fennel, and wild day lilies thrive there, year after year. The spirit of John Appleseed lives in them.